HAIR DANCE!

words by

DINAH JOHNSON

photographs by

KELLY JOHNSON

HENRY HOLT AND COMPANY   NEW YORK

For some special little sisters: Olania Washington, Angel Sledge, Malyka Norville, Evan Bowman, Jasmine Gordon, Bria McKenzie, Taja Geiger, Marley Thomson, Jaden Parker, Carlisle and Chandler Cooper, Jahnyah Francis, Nyah Taylor-Butcher, and, as always, for Taelor Johnson and Niani Feelings
—D. J.

For my lovely daughters, Natasha and Nicole, and for my mother, Gloria Dean Tims, who carries on our family legacy with grace
—K. J.

Thanks to Thiel Johnson, Kimberly Brown, and Kay Dean Toran.
Thank you to Dinah Johnson and to Laura Godwin, Caroline Meckler, and Laurent Linn.
Special thanks to Nicole Johnson, Nyasha Bryant, Alexandra Rossi, Keyaira Rentie, Furaha-Esube, Regan Mims, Lavosha Baker, Zoie Sheng, Ashley Strader, Miranda Streeter, Kaelin Pierce, Mariah Jackson, Jacci Walker, Mariah and Marquiah Ladd, Kieara Loving, Nina Stewart, Jasmine Barber, Asasia Richardson, Madison Hairston, Marlicia McDonald, Sanari Roberson, and Aliyah Williams.

Henry Holt and Company, LLC
Publishers since 1866
175 Fifth Avenue
New York, New York 10010
www.henryholtchildrensbooks.com

Henry Holt® is a registered trademark of Henry Holt and Company, LLC.
Text copyright © 2007 by Dinah Johnson
Photographs copyright © 2007 by Kelly Johnson
Library of Congress Cataloging-in-Publication Data
Johnson, Dinah.
Hair dance! / by Dinah Johnson; photographs by Kelly Johnson.—1st ed.
p.   cm.
Includes bibliographical references.
ISBN-13: 978-0-8050-6523-7 / ISBN-10: 0-8050-6523-7
[1. Hair—Fiction.] I. Johnson, Kelly, ill. II. Title.
PS3560.O3747H35 2007   811'.54—dc22   2006030616

First Edition—2007
Book design and hand lettering by Laurent Linn
Printed in China on acid-free paper. ∞

10 9 8 7 6 5 4 3 2 1

PHOTOGRAPHER'S INTRODUCTION

My love of hair goes back to my grandparents Benjamin and Mary Rose Dean, who dreamed of owning a successful business doing what they enjoyed: hairstyling. Though my grandparents are no longer with us, the salon they founded in 1954, Dean's Beauty Salon & Barber Shop, has remained in the family (my mother is the owner, and my sister is the manager) and has continued to flourish for more than fifty years.

As a child, I worked in the shop. I would take out rollers, clean combs and brushes, and get lunch for the staff and clients. In my spare moments, I watched as men, women, and children got "beautified" (as my grandmother always said) and was in awe of the contribution my grandparents made to their family and community. A visit to the salon lifts the spirit and moves the soul. It creates an energy—coolness, beauty, movement, and pride.

My pride in my grandparents' legacy was the inspiration for this book. Hair is our crowning glory, and every day we should appreciate its grace, color, and texture. I wanted to portray African American hair in the most radiant light, as my grandparents did.

The girls I photographed are the ones who truly give life to this book. They have wonderful talents, and I couldn't have asked for better models. *Positive, unique, glamorous,* and *elegant* are the words I'd use to describe them, and my only hope is that girls who read this book will envision for themselves a bright future.

—KELLY JOHNSON

We play beauty parlor
every day
styling hair
in all kinds of ways

It's sassy short
and bouncy long
barrettes on my braids
keep the beat of the song

It's a wind song
a hair song

Camera's just about to click
strike a pose in red

showing off my Afro puffs
proud and pretty on my head

Braids swing with me
like water, moving free
no matter how I wear my hair
it's a special part of me

Special like my friends—
come on, you'll fit right in
with our rainbow tribe
of heritage
our sisterhood of hearts

People stare at my hair

sometimes—

it looks like

a work of art

and inside

I sing

It's a hair song

For my
Afro halo heavenly hair

My nature hair
real hair
flower power strong hair

Strong hair growing
into dreadlocks
(caring hands
make them love locs)

Mama's hands snap pictures
we can keep forever
of hair framing faces
full of friendship

Hats framing faces
full of happy

Heart happy
hair happy

Braids fly high into sky

In a jump dance
street dance
friends dance
feet dance—

HAIR
DANCE!

WRITER'S NOTE

The girls and ladies in my life have hair that is every length, every color, every texture. We love our hair plain and pretty, or adorned with cowrie shells and hair jewelry. Hair—and how we care for it and for each other—is one of our most important links to the African heritages from which we descend. Our culture values beauty and improvisation in every realm of life, and hair is no exception. So we work with it, play with it, style it, and treasure it as the Art that it is.

—DINAH JOHNSON

To read more about hair and its history—in some ways it embodies the history of a whole people—look for these books:

FOR THE LITTLE SISTERS

It's All Good Hair: The Guide to Styling and Grooming Black Children's Hair by Michele N-K. Collison (Amistad, 2002).

Kids Talk Hair: An Instruction Book for Grown-Ups and Kids by Pamela Ferrell (Cornrows and Company, 1999).

Kinki Kreations: A Parent's Guide to Natural Black Hair Care for Kids by Jena Renee Williams (Harlem Moon, 2004).

Wavy, Curly, Kinky: The African American Child's Hair Care Guide by Deborah R. Lilly (Wiley, 2005).

FOR THE LADIES

Bulletproof Diva: Tales of Race, Sex, and Hair by Lisa Jones (Anchor, 1997).

Hair Matters: Beauty, Power and Black Women's Consciousness by Ingrid Banks (New York University Press, 2000).

Hair Raising: Beauty, Culture, and African American Women by Noliwe M. Rooks (Rutgers University Press, 1996).

Hair Story: Untangling the Roots of Black Hair in America by Ayana D. Byrd and Lori L. Tharps (St. Martin's, 2002).

On Her Own Ground: The Life and Times of Madam C. J. Walker by A'Lelia Bundles (Scribner, 2002).

Tenderheaded: A Comb-Bending Collection of Hair Stories by Pamela Johnson and Juliette Harris (Washington Square Press, 2002).